THOMAS KINKADE

with Anne Christian Buchanan

Warmth from the Windows

Harvest House Publishers
Eugene, Oregon

Warmth from the Windows

Text Copyright © 2001 by Media Arts Group, Inc., Morgan Hill, CA 95037
and Harvest House Publishers, Eugene, OR 97402

Kinkade, Thomas, 1958-
     Warmth from the windows / Thomas Kinkade.
         p.cm. — (Simpler times collection)
     ISPN 0-7369-0636-3
     1. Home. 2. Family. 3. Simplicity. 4. Quality of life. I. Title.

     HQ734 .K4835 2001
     306 — dc21

2001024260

Text for this book has been excerpted from *Simpler Times* by Thomas
Kinkade (Harvest House Publishers, 1996).

Verses are taken from the Holy Bible, New International Version®.
Copyright © 1973, 1978, 1984 by the International Bible Society.
Used by permission of Zondervan Publishing House.

Design and production by Koechel Peterson & Associates, Minneapolis, Minnesota

Thus, simply as a little child,

we learn a home is made from love.

Warm as the golden hearthfire on the floor.

—AUTHOR UNKNOWN

Someone asked me once why I paint so many houses and cottages with warm, glowing windows. At first I didn't know what to say. After all, how does an artist explain why he paints what he does?

I've thought a lot about that question, though, and now I think I have an answer. I paint glowing windows because glowing windows say home to me. Glowing windows say welcome. They say all is well. They say that someone's waiting, someone cares enough to turn a light on.

For a person like me, who grew up in a single-parent household and often had to come home to an empty house, that "someone's home" glow is irresistible. It draws the eye like a brightly wrapped present, a promise of wonderful secrets inside. Can you see a brightly lit window without even the smallest urge to go peek in, to see what the people are doing and what their lives are like? I can't either.

In fact, as I am dabbing brushfuls of golden paint on those windows—whether on a rambling Victorian mansion or a tiny little fishing cabin—I am always imagining a world of family gatherings, of quiet times spent in the company of loved ones.

There is nothing like staying at home for real comfort.

—JANE AUSTEN

An elegant sufficiency, content, retirement, rural quiet, friendship, books, ea...

and alternate labour, useful life, progressive virtue, and approving Heave...

—JAMES THOMSO...

I can almost smell the toasty aromas of popcorn or a pie baking. I can hear the lively sounds of laughter and perhaps the tinkle of a music box. I can feel the plush and silky textures of a velvet settee and a baby's cheek. And I see it all lit by the golden glow of a fireplace or a candle or a lamp with a fringed shade.

I paint warm windows, in other words, because I envision a perpetual warm reunion.

I have that same feeling every night when I leave my studio. I love to close my studio door and make my way across the small lawn, up the stone steps, across the patio to our kitchen door.

Outside, all is dark. But through the glowing kitchen window I can see Nanette moving back and forth, singing gently as she adds the last touches to our dinner. And I can imagine what else is going on inside.

Seven-year-old Merritt is lifting the lid to the pot of soup and stirring while she tells her mother about her new pet snail. (It's in a jar by the door, waiting for me to see.) Five-year-old Chandler is perched on a stool, "helping," determined to do whatever her big sister does. Baby Winsor in her high chair is grinning her two-toothed grin through a mouthful of sweet potatoes.

And around it all there is the warm glow of anticipation.

I'm on my way home. And I know what will happen next. The girls will race to the door to grab my knees and jump in my arms and show me their snail. Nanette will give me a kiss. Winsor will grin and blow bubbles.

We'll eat. And then we'll play. And then we'll read together and bundle the children off to bed after listening to their good night prayers. There will be time for Nanette and me to sit and talk awhile.

This is my home, my welcoming world. This is my anchor, the resting place for my heart. These times together are what put the glow in my windows.

But the interaction in our house is not always gentle and serene. It's just as likely to be rambunctious and rowdy. The pillows of our large family room sofas get thrown a lot during our family gymnastics sessions. We roll on the floor; we wrestle. The girls play "Hop on Pop," which means they sit on my chest and bounce up and down like kangaroos. (I can already see that this game will have an age limit.)

Little things seem nothing, but they give peace,
like those meadow flowers which individually
seem odorless but all together perfume the air.

—GEORGE BERNANOS

These are wonderful times we have together, full of the innocence of childhood and the warmth of family togetherness. The girls love those times. Nanette and I love them, too. We love being able to tumble around on the rug together. We love feeling breathless with laughter and love.

In our house, we know each other. We talk a lot. We know where each other is ticklish. We read together from children's books or from our big family Bible. We paint together, although our styles are different. (My style is a highly romanticized form of realism; the girls are still largely in their abstract period!)

We play games in our house. Merritt is just now learning checkers, and I look forward to the day she can play a heated Monopoly match with me. We sing songs—making up in enthusiasm for what we lack in talent.

We also love to bring our friends into the warm circle of the light in our home. We let the kids run wild in the rumpus room while the grown-ups relax and enjoy each other's company. Sometimes we play board games. Sometimes we all go out to dinner together or take a walk in the neighborhood. Mostly, though, we just sit and talk.

...that we may live peaceful and quiet

lives in all godliness and holiness.

—1 TIMOTHY 2:2

Ever since Nanette and I met at age thirteen, we have had a dream of creating a home together—a haven where we could live and raise our children. As our lives have moved forward, we have fought to hold on to that peaceful vision. Its details have changed, but not its central character. Again and again we have tried to make choices that would help us find a resting place for our hearts.

For instance, we've taken every opportunity to avoid spending sizable chunks of our lives simply moving from one place to another. Our current home was chosen with exactly that vision in mind. Our house was built in an earlier era and is located an easy walk or bike ride away from the village center. That village is where we shop and go on dates together and take our kids to school. Whenever we can, we walk or ride bikes to do our errands, turning necessary chores into family outings. And we've managed to all but eliminate a commute to work. When the opportunity came, we purchased the cottage next door and converted it into a studio. That decision grants daily rewards as I make my thirty-second commute through the redwoods, as Nanette comes over to stretch canvases and talk, as my daughters crash through the door after school to share their latest news.

Hospitality: a little fire, a little food,

and an immense quiet.

—RALPH WALDO EMERSON

His house was perfect, whether you liked food, or sleep, or work, or story-telli

or singing, or just sitting and thinking, best, or a pleasant mixture of them

—J.R.R. TOLKI

THE HOB.

Another battle we have chosen to opt out of is the information revolution. We don't surf the Net. We don't follow CNN. In fact, we've chosen to keep television out of our house entirely. This is not because we are opposed to the medium of television, but because we are opposed to what television tends to do in our lives. In our experience, television is a thief that robs us of our time together and steals our peace.

When we are watching TV, we are not riding our bikes or playing in the yard or having couch-pillow fights with our girls in the living room. Instead, we are soaking up the subtle and not-so-subtle messages that we should want more, more, more...and sacrifice our peace if necessary to obtain it.

In fact, saying no to the messages of our surrounding culture is a choice I try to make almost every day. The word *no* has become a real lifesaver to me, and I use it without guilt. More often than not, in my experience, using the word *yes* in response to the world around me generates a harvest of chaos. The word *no*, on the other hand, generates a great harvest of peace in our lives.

Art can only be truly Art by presenting an adequate outward symbol of some fact of the interior life.

—MARGARET FULLER

Home!…how much it all meant to him, and the special value of some such anchorage in one's existence…. It was good to think he had this to come back to, this place which was all his own, these things which were so glad to see him again and could always be counted upon for the same simple welcome.

—KENNETH GRAHAME

THE WIND IN THE WILLOWS

He makes me lie down in green pas

he leads me beside quiet w

he restores m

— PSALM

For example, I have learned to say no to commitments that steal away our family time and eat into my painting time. I find myself practicing that word *no* on a daily basis:

"No, I can't have visitors today."

"No, I can't attend that meeting. I spend my evenings with my family."

"No, I can't grant that interview. I need to paint today."

And of course, I need to say no to myself as well, at times.

No isn't always an easy or comfortable choice. Most of us are so accustomed to overstimulation that quiet feels strange to us; it makes us nervous. Quiet can be an acquired taste, especially in a society that revels in complexity.

But what an improvement when we finally begin to feel at home with a calmer way of life. What a sense of empowerment when we realize we can say no to the constant bombardment of our minds and senses. What a surge of energy when we realize that saying no is really a way of saying yes to all we really care about.

I want to say yes, for example, to deep and intimate relationships. And I would far rather invest my energy in maintaining a vital marriage and raising well-loved children than in getting ahead and creating an empire. I believe that how I treat my family, how I spend my time with them, has eternal implications. So I want to feel assured that I am influencing their life for the better. I want to teach them, tickle them, discipline them, hug them. I want to know what they're reading, what they're learning, what they're wondering about.

I am willing to say no to a lot of things—to say yes to my family in that way.

I also want to say yes to experiences, to surprise, to serendipity—all the things that have no room to happen if I'm saying yes to the demands of all the world around me. I want to experience my life rather than spend it on a treadmill with the rest of the rat race. And that, too, means I have to say no to a lot of good things that take my time. It means I must give up some opportunities, take off the get-ahead blinders, make space in my life for experiences to happen.

The more one does and sees and feels, the more one is able to do, and the more genuine may be one's appreciation of fundamental things like home, and love, and understanding companionship.

—AMELIA EARHART

21

Yes, I make plans. Yes, I have goals. But stopping to examine a bug with my five-year-old may well reap more long-term rewards than beating a deadline.

Conversation, too, is what I imagine going on behind the glowing windows in my paintings. Lively conversation—about books, about old movies, about hopes, and dreams, and the many blessings God gives us. Conversation that can occupy a whole evening. Conversation where people's lives touch in a meaningful way.

That kind of conversation has almost become a lost art in our high-tech age. We became aware of this loss during a summer we spent in a little English village. There, social activity is built around the town pub. People gather there to eat a simple meal or drink the famous English ale, but mostly to talk and laugh.

The sun at home warms better than the sun elsewhere.

—ALBANIAN PROVERB

remember, I remember, the house where I was born,

he little window where the sun came peeping in at morn…

—THOMAS HOOD

Thomas
Kinkade

Here in America, we've installed television sets everywhere so that people never have to converse. Even restaurants have given in to this trend, and it is often difficult to find a table where you can escape the distracting glare of a television set. Have you ever walked at night by a window where the television was on? The light is dim and cold. But walk at night by a window where a fire is flickering, where a candle is lit, and see the difference. The warm glow in the windows is so inviting that it draws you in.

It's not high-tech entertainment that puts the warmth in the windows, but human connection. It's human warmth that makes up the golden glow. And I think that most of us are instinctively drawn to that warmth.

And yet the glow in the windows is not reserved solely for families like mine. The warmth is not exclusive, not unreachable. The windows can shine wherever you find a resting place for your heart.

I think of my mother. She and my father parted ways when I was very young, and she has lived alone for nearly twenty years, since the day my brother and I left for college. And yet her house always glows with that "someone's home" light because my mother, more than almost anyone I know, is serenely at home with herself.

Every inch of her house tells a tale of her busy and involved life. Tangled skeins of yarn bear testimony to the cat's good time, and gardening tools lean in a corner of her garage. Projects sprawl on the tables, waiting for her attention, and pencils and notebooks are everywhere, filled with her notes and observations. My mother's cozy little nest is every inch her own; to me it exudes the same welcoming glow that my own home holds.

You can put that same light in your windows by surrounding yourself with your work and your play and your memories. If you love art, cover your walls with paintings or prints that speak to your soul and bring you peace. If you love music, put the piano in the center of the room and keep the stereo tuned to your favorite station. Pad the sofa with fluffy pillows. Drape a soft afghan on your favorite chair—and put a favorite book nearby. And yes, you might want to light a candle on the windowsill.

You also put the light in your windows by sharing your life with others. Invite neighbors or friends for an evening of checkers or chamber music or conversation, giving them a taste of your life.

Make it your ambition to lead a quiet life....

—1 THESSALONIANS 4:11

But most of all, you put a light in the window by coming home to yourself. By becoming friends with who you are and who you can be. By finding a resting place for your heart.

My constant prayer is that my work will inspire others with a vision of how good life can be. And time and time again, God has graciously given me evidence of the fruits of my labor. At a recent visit to a gallery, I was approached by a woman whose story touched my heart.

"Mr. Kinkade?" she began hesitantly. "I just wanted to tell you what this painting did for me." The print she was pointing to showed a cozy little thatched cottage surrounded by bright, exuberant gardens. "Because I feel as though it saved my life."

Naturally enough, this dramatic statement caught my attention, and I spent the next few minutes listening to the woman's story. She told of a life broken by the pain of loss, of a hopelessness so complete that she eventually decided she couldn't go on living. But then a tiny spark of possibility was struck. While she sat in the doctor's office, she found her eyes drawn to a print on the wall—the same print she was pointing to now. And as she phrased it to me, "It was like I was wandering down the little path, smelling the flowers.

And I just knew what was inside—I could see the little rocking chair, the book beside it, and it was all so peaceful. I'm saving my money for my own little place with a garden—just like the garden in the picture. Before, I never thought something like that was possible for someone like me. But when I saw that painting, I got a glimpse of hope—of a world where I could be happy again."

As that woman ended her story, she told of the new life she had built for herself. "My whole world is brighter now," she concluded.

Needless to say, that conversation affected me more deeply than I can express. It reminded me of the need that people have for a bit of light and warmth in their lives—and the healing power that can come from a little spark of hope.

After all, my painting didn't save that woman's life. The painting was only a catalyst, a starting point that began the process of rekindling hope in her heart. She took it from there, nursing that little spark into a cozy fire that lit the windows of her life.

Where thou art, that is home.

—EMILY DICKINSON

Home is where the heart is,

The soul's bright guiding star.

Home is where real love is,

Where our own dear ones are.

Home means someone waiting

To give a welcome smile.

Home means peace

and joy and rest

And everything worthwhile.

—ANONYMOUS